ALL AROUND THE WORLD
SAUDI ARABIA

by Kristine Spanier, MLIS

pogo

Ideas for Parents and Teachers

Pogo Books let children practice reading informational text while introducing them to nonfiction features such as headings, labels, sidebars, maps, and diagrams, as well as a table of contents, glossary, and index.

Carefully leveled text with a strong photo match offers early fluent readers the support they need to succeed.

Before Reading

- "Walk" through the book and point out the various nonfiction features. Ask the student what purpose each feature serves.
- Look at the glossary together. Read and discuss the words.

Read the Book

- Have the child read the book independently.
- Invite him or her to list questions that arise from reading.

After Reading

- Discuss the child's questions. Talk about how he or she might find answers to those questions.
- Prompt the child to think more. Ask: Saudi Arabia doesn't have any rivers! Do you live near rivers?

Pogo Books are published by Jump!
5357 Penn Avenue South
Minneapolis, MN 55419
www.jumplibrary.com

Library of Congress Cataloging-in-Publication Data

Names: Spanier, Kristine, author.
Title: Saudi Arabia / Kristine Spanier.
Description: Minneapolis, MN: Jump!, Inc., 2021.
Series: All around the world | Includes index.
Audience: 7-10 | Audience: 2-3
Identifiers: LCCN 2019047586 (print)
LCCN 2019047587 (ebook)
ISBN 9781645273530 (hardcover)
ISBN 9781645273547 (paperback)
ISBN 9781645273554 (ebook)
Subjects: LCSH: Saudi Arabia—Juvenile literature.
Classification: LCC DS204.25 .S63 2021 (print)
LCC DS204.25 (ebook) | DDC 953.8—dc23
LC record available at https://lccn.loc.gov/2019047586
LC ebook record available at https://lccn.loc.gov/2019047587

Editor: Jenna Gleisner
Designer: Molly Ballanger

Photo Credits: Gimas/Shutterstock, cover; ZouZou/Shutterstock, 1; Pixfiction/Shutterstock, 3; wajedram/iStock, 4t; Vigen M/Shutterstock, 4b; irisphoto2/iStock, 5; Anadolu Agency/Getty, 6-7; afby71/Getty, 8-9; Mlenny/iStock, 10; Shazrul Edwan/Shutterstock, 11; Almalki-photo/iStock, 12-13; StuPorts/iStock, 14-15tl; Ivkuzmin/Dreamstime, 14-15tr; Agami Photo Agency/Shutterstock, 14-15bl; Roland Seitre/Minden Pictures/SuperStock, 14-15br; Rawpixel/iStock, 16; FAYEZ NURELDINE/Getty, 17; Ahmed Hamdy Hassan/Shutterstock, 18-19; World In Focus Photography/Alamy, 20-21; tanukiphoto/iStock, 23.

Printed in the United States of America at Corporate Graphics in North Mankato, Minnesota.

TABLE OF CONTENTS

CHAPTER 1

WELCOME TO SAUDI ARABIA!

Would you like to try kabsa? This is a dish made with meat and rice. Shwarma is roasted meat. Where can you taste these foods? Saudi Arabia!

kabsa

shwarma

Go to a camel race!
Windsurf in the
Red Sea. Welcome!

The **capital** is Riyadh. A king rules the country. He makes all of the decisions and laws. The king is from the House of Saud. This is the **royal** family. The men in the family choose a new king.

WHAT DO YOU THINK?

Women here have few **rights**. They cannot lead the country. They cannot travel or work without permission. Do you think women and men should be treated equally? Why or why not?

Crown Prince Mohammed bin Salman

King Salman of Saudi Arabia

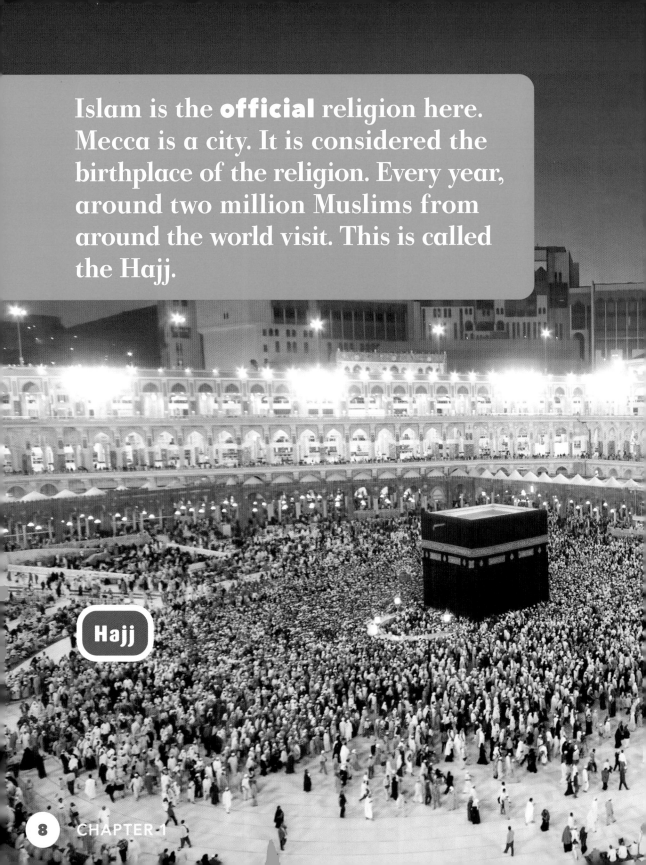

Islam is the **official** religion here. Mecca is a city. It is considered the birthplace of the religion. Every year, around two million Muslims from around the world visit. This is called the Hajj.

Hajj

TAKE A LOOK!

Most Saudi Arabians dress in **traditional** clothing.
What do they wear?

HIJAB
(veil over head)

NIQAB
(face cover)

THAWB
(shirt)

ABAYA
(black cloak)

SIRWAL
(pants)

WOMEN

'IQAL
(cord around
head cover)

KAFFIYEH
(head cover)

THAWB
(long cloak)

MEN

CHAPTER 2

LAND AND ANIMALS

The Rub' al-Khali is in the south. It is part of the Arabian Desert. Temperatures can rise above 130 degrees Fahrenheit (54 degrees Celsius) here!

Arabian Desert

dates

This is the largest country in the world with no rivers. This makes farming **crops** difficult. Some fields are **irrigated**. Important crops are dates, wheat, melons, and potatoes.

Temperatures are cooler in the **highlands**. Sometimes it even snows! Mount Sawda is the highest point here. It is more than 10,250 feet (3,124 meters) high.

highlands

caracal

white-tailed mongoose

desert hedgehog

Arabian wolf

Many animals are found in the mountain region. Why? There are more plants to eat! Some animals **thrive** in the desert. The caracal is one. The white-tailed mongoose and desert hedgehog live here, too. Keep an eye out for the Arabian wolf!

DID YOU KNOW?

Most desert animals are **nocturnal**. Why? The sun and sand get too hot during the day!

CHAPTER 3

LIFE IN SAUDI ARABIA

People here celebrate Eid al-Fitr. They spend time with family. Children receive gifts. Families help the needy during Eid al-Adha.

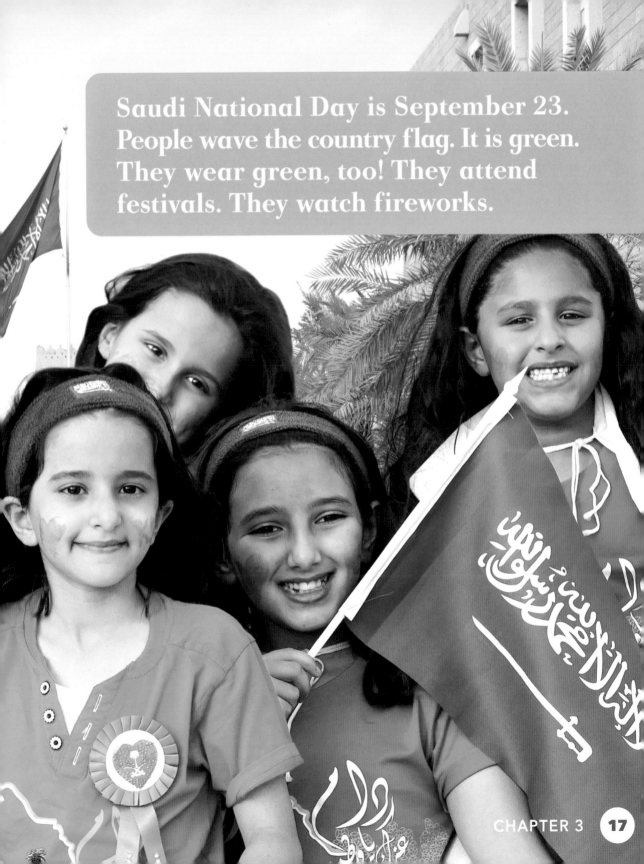

Saudi National Day is September 23. People wave the country flag. It is green. They wear green, too! They attend festivals. They watch fireworks.

Children go to school for 12 years. Religion is an important subject. Girls and boys are in separate classes after second grade. High schoolers have a choice. They may continue a general education. Or they can study to prepare for jobs.

WHAT DO YOU THINK?

Are girls and boys in separate classrooms where you go to school? If not, what would you like about this? What wouldn't you like about it?

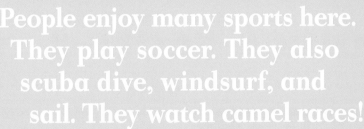

People enjoy many sports here.
They play soccer. They also
scuba dive, windsurf, and
sail. They watch camel races!

There is a lot to see
in this interesting land.
Would you like to visit?

QUICK FACTS & TOOLS

SAUDI ARABIA

Location: Middle East

Size: 830,000 square miles (2,149,690 square kilometers)

Population: 33,091,113 (July 2018 estimate)

Capital: Riyadh

Type of Government: absolute monarchy

Language: Arabic

Exports: petroleum and petroleum products

Currency: Saudi riyal

GLOSSARY

capital: A city where government leaders meet.

crops: Plants grown for food.

highlands: Areas of land that are elevated or mountainous.

irrigated: Supplied with water by artificial means, such as channels and pipes.

nocturnal: Active at night.

official: Having the approval of an authority or public body.

rights: Things you are legally or morally entitled to do.

royal: Relating to or belonging to a king or queen or a member of his or her family.

thrive: To do well or become strong and healthy.

traditional: Having to do with the customs, beliefs, or activities that are handed down from one generation to the next.

Saudi Arabia's currency

INDEX

TO LEARN MORE

Finding more information is as easy as 1, 2, 3.

1. Go to www.factsurfer.com
2. Enter "SaudiArabia" into the search box.
3. Click the "Surf" button to see a list of websites.

FACT SURFER